SCHOLASTIC
LITERATURE GUIDE
GRADES 4–8

The Lord of the Rings

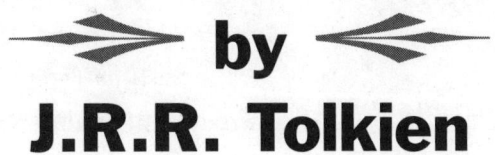

by

J.R.R. Tolkien

Written by Denise Kiernan
Cover design by Vincent Ceci and Jaime Lucero
Interior design by Robert Dominguez and Jaime Lucero for Grafica, Inc.
Original cover and interior design by Drew Hines
Interior illustrations by Teresa Southwell
Photo research by Sarah Longacre

Author photo on page 4 by AP Wide World Photos.

ISBN 0-439-41129-7
Copyright © 2002 by Scholastic Inc.
All rights reserved.
Printed in the U.S.A.

1 2 3 4 5 6 7 8 9 10   40   08 07 06 05 04 03 02

Table of Contents

Before Reading the Book

SUMMARY

Hobbit Bilbo Baggins holds a birthday party for his young cousin Frodo and himself and says farewell to friends as he prepares to leave the Shire. Among the possessions that Bilbo leaves with Frodo is a magic ring of invisibility that carries with it a great deal of power—and immense danger. The great wizard Gandalf tells Frodo that the ring must be destroyed; Frodo must take the ring far from his home in the Shire to protect its inhabitants. Gandalf also warns Frodo that he must be careful not to fall under the ring's power because it will ultimately destroy whoever possesses it. Frodo has no idea that his quest to destroy the ring will take him on an epic adventure through Middle-earth. He will be put to incredible tests of spirit, heart, and mind.

Along with his hobbit friends Sam, Merry, and Pippin, Frodo goes to Rivendell, where a council has been convened. The council agrees that the One Ring in Frodo's possession must be destroyed in the only way possible—it must be returned to the fires of the volcano of Mt. Doom where it was forged. Frodo must take it there, but he and his companions must also evade those who seek the ring's power for themselves, including Sauron, the Dark Lord of Mordor, who made the ring and wants to use it to control Middle-earth; Saruman, once a great wizard and chief of Gandalf's order, now obsessed with the power the ring can give him; and Gollum, a decrepit creature and former hobbit, who once possessed the ring and suffered for it. Gollum now thinks of nothing else but getting the ring back.

Through battles, attacks, and tests of will, Frodo and his friends are successful in their quest: Evil forces are faced, good prevails, and the One Ring is destroyed. After passing on the responsibility of writing the history of the times to his friend Sam—the same responsibility that was passed to him by his cousin Bilbo—Frodo is carried away from the Shire toward the Blessed Realm. After seeing him off, Sam, Merry, and Pippin return home to the Shire.

STORY CHARACTERS

The Fellowship: Those Who Went Forth from Rivendell

Frodo Baggins, a hobbit and holder of the One Ring

Samwise Gamgee, a hobbit and Frodo's gardener and faithful companion

Peregrin Took (Pippin) and Meriadoc Brandybuck (Merry), hobbits and good friends of Frodo

Gandalf, a great wizard

Gimli, a dwarf, son of Glóin

Boromir, son of Denethor, the steward of Gondor; brother of Faramir

Aragorn (Strider), chieftain of the Dúnedain and rightful heir to the throne of Gondor

Legolas, a brave elf and friend of Gimli

Others—Hobbits, Elves, Dwarves, Men, Animals, Ents, Orcs, Monsters, and Such

Arwen Evenstar, an elf, daughter of Elrond and Celebrian

Bilbo Baggins, a hobbit who passes the One Ring to his cousin Frodo Baggins

Lobelia Sackville-Baggins, cousin of Bilbo Baggins

Lotho Sackville-Baggins, son of Lobelia Baggins who eventually becomes an ally of Saruman

Balin, a dwarf who aids Bilbo

Balrog, a horrible monster of fire and shadows

Bard, a man who saves Lake-town by killing the dragon Smaug

Barliman Butterbur, the innkeeper of *The Prancing Pony*

Barrow-wights, evil spirits from Angmar

Beregond, a soldier of Gondo who takes care of Pippin

Fredegar Bolger, a hobbit and friend to Frodo

Tom Bombadil, husband of Goldberry and master of the Old Forest

Celeborn, lord of the elves

Círdan, an elf and Lord of the Grey Havens

Farmer Cotton, a hobbit and father of Rosie Cotton

Rosie Cotton, a hobbit who marries Sam Gamgee

Dáin, cousin of Thorin Oakenshield

Dead Men, cursed Men of the White Mountains who break their oath of allegiance to Isildur

Denethor, steward of Gondor, father of Boromir and Faramir

STORY CHARACTERS (continued)

Elbereth Gilthoniel, queen of the Valar

Elendil, founder of the kingdoms of Arnor and Gondor, father of Isildur and Anárion

Elrond, an elf, father of Arwen, and husband of Celebrían

Ents, creatures that look like a cross between men and trees

Eomer, nephew of King Théoden, brother of Éowyn

Eowyn, niece of King Théoden, sister of Éomer

Faramir, son of Denethor, steward of Gondor; brother of Boromir

Bill Ferny, a man who spies for Saruman

Galadriel, lady of the elves

Gildor, a high elf who serves Elrond

Glóin, a dwarf and old friend of Bilbo, father of Gimli

Glorfindel, a great elf lord and one of the chiefs of Rivendell

Goldberry, wife of Tom Bombadil who has power over rainfall

Gollum (Sméagol), once a hobbit, now a decrepit creature obsessed with the Ring

Grima (Wormtongue), a servant of Saruman

Gwaihir, lord of the eagles

Haldir, an elf of Lothlórien

Isildur, son of Elendil who cut the One Ring from Sauron's hand

Nazgúl (Ring-wraith), a servant of Sauron

Orcs, violent creatures also called goblins

Ted Sandyman, a miller

Saruman, a wizard of Gandalf's order who falls under the evil influence of the Ring

Sauron, the maker of the One Ring and Dark Lord of Mordor

Shadowfax, a great and powerful horse

Shelob, a giant spider

Théoden, King of Rohan

Thorin Oakenshield, son of the King of the Dwarves

Treebeard (Fangorn), an ent, the oldest living thing in Middle-earth

Wargs, evil wolves

ABOUT THE AUTHOR

J.R.R. Tolkien was born in 1892 in South Africa and grew up in Birmingham, England. Tolkien left Oxford University to serve in World War I. He returned to receive his Master of Arts from the prestigious university in 1919. A writer and teacher for all of his life, Tolkien's love for and incredible knowledge of languages led him to work on the famed *Oxford English Dictionary*, and he eventually became a professor of Anglo-Saxon at Oxford. When Tolkien published his first novel, *The Hobbit*, at age 45, it immediately received both popular and critical acclaim. He then worked on *The Lord of the Rings* from 1936 to 1949. Although he published many other books in his lifetime, *The Hobbit* and *The Lord of the Rings* are still immensely popular, and Tolkien remains an icon; his books have spawned clubs, web sites, and societies dedicated to studying the world he created. Perhaps the most recent sign of the remarkable popularity of *The Lord of the Rings* is the making of three films, one for each part of the trilogy, to be released in three consecutive years beginning in December of 2001. J.R.R. Tolkien died in 1973, and several of his books, including *The Silmarillion*, have been published posthumously.

LITERATURE CONNECTIONS

Other books by J.R.R. Tolkien include:

- *The Hobbit*
- *The Silmarillion*
- *The Adventures of Tom Bombadil*
- *Leaf by Niggle*
- *The Father Christmas Letters*

VOCABULARY

Assign the following words from the book to individual students, or groups of students. After students look up their assigned words in the dictionary, instruct them to do the following:

1. Write the definition(s) of the word.
2. Use it in a sentence.
3. Give any other forms of the word (if, for example, it may also be used as an adjective or verb as well as a noun).

Students can then share their findings with the rest of the class, and their combined efforts can be compiled, copied, and used as a vocabulary builder and reference for the class. As students read the book, encourage them to write down unfamiliar words. These words should be added to the class vocabulary builder and reference guide.

In addition to learning new English vocabulary words, another exciting challenge for students is discovering the style of language that Tolkien created for his books. While addressing general vocabulary, you may also want to discuss Tolkien's use of language and the alphabet he created. *NOTE: Discuss with your students the differences between American English and British English spellings (for example, color and colour, valor and valour). The words listed below appear as they do in the book.*

THINKING ABOUT THEMES

malice	chasm	shrouded	dismay	brazen
trifle	sunder	vigour	rending	clamouring
wayfarer	wane	rouse	kindred	aghast
perish	lineage	treachery	desolation	sullen
laden	hither	brandish	concourse	ruffian
unscathed	tidings	vigilance	haven	outlandish
assail	amiss	stagnant	tumult	lore
anvil	vanquish	remorse	renowned	wrought
adamant	keen	crevice	burnish	
realm	rash	daunt	unkempt	

Before students begin to read the book, discuss the idea of themes with them. Some themes to keep in mind while reading *The Lord of the Rings* include the following:
- Power. What is power? Does power always corrupt or do damage? Can absolute power be used for good?
- Tolkien's use of light and dark as representations of good and evil.
- The idea of destiny as opposed to free will.

GETTING STARTED
Use one or more of these ideas to introduce the book to the class.
- Write the word *quest* on the board. Question students about their ideas of what quest is. Have they read other books or stories or seen films about quests?
- Ask students to look at the individual book and chapter titles. What images and ideas do the titles summon?
- The appendices to *The Lord of the Rings* are a book unto themselves! Have students look through the timeline, language description, family trees, and maps. What kind of world do students predict they will encounter in the book?

NOTE: Activities and reproducibles are cumulative in nature. Although the focus in the discussion of the second and third books is on information that specifically appears in these books, it also builds upon aspects brought to light in the prior books.

WHEN BOOKS ARE MADE INTO MOVIES
Students may have seen or heard about the movies that are based on *The Lord of the Rings*. Encourage those who have seen the film to note the differences they find between it and the book. Do they think the movie is true to Tolkien's work? Remind students that the images they conjure up in their minds, thanks to Tolkien's remarkable description and detail, may be far more wonderful—and different—than what appears in the movie.

Exploring the Book

WHAT HAPPENS

The Fellowship of the Ring begins in the Shire at the joint birthday party of hobbits Bilbo Baggins (age 111) and his cousin, Frodo (age 33). After the party, Bilbo says good-bye to the Shire and passes on many possessions to Frodo, including a ring of invisibility. Bilbo is reluctant to turn over the ring but finally accedes to the wizard Gandalf's wishes to do so. Many years later, Gandalf explains the story of the ring to Frodo. Sauron, the Dark Lord of Mordor, made the ring and wants to use its power to control the inhabitants of Middle-earth. Gollum has told Sauron that a hobbit has the ring. Gandalf warns Frodo that the ring will eventually destroy anyone who wears it. The ring can only be destroyed if someone throws it into the fires from which it was forged, the volcano of Orodruin or Mt. Doom. Frodo, and hobbits Sam, Merry, and Pippin set out for Rivendell with the ring. Sinister Black Riders track the hobbits, but they're helped by others, including Farmer Maggot, the elf Glorfindel, and Goldberry and her husband Tom Bombadil. At *The Prancing Pony* inn, the hobbits meet the mysterious Strider, who turns out to be a friend of Gandalf's. Strider guides the hobbits on their journey to Rivendell. At the end of Book One, a wounded Frodo lies unconscious after another narrow escape from the Black Riders.

QUESTIONS TO TALK ABOUT

COMPREHENSION AND RECALL

1. What is being celebrated at the beginning of *The Fellowship of the Ring*? (*It is the joint birthday party of Bilbo and Frodo Baggins, and Bilbo is saying good-bye to his home in the Shire.*)

2. What does the ring's maker wish to do with the ring? (*Sauron, the Dark Lord of Mordor, hopes to control Middle-earth with the ring's power.*)

3. What is the only way the One Ring can be destroyed? (*It must be returned to the fires from which it was forged in the volcano, Mt. Doom.*)

HIGHER-LEVEL THINKING SKILLS

4. What does Bilbo's reaction to Gandalf's instruction that he hand over the ring to Frodo say about the ring itself? (*Bilbo is reluctant to part with the ring, and this shows the power that the ring has over its bearer.*)

5. Why does Gandalf refuse the ring when Frodo offers it to him? (*He is afraid that its power will corrupt him.*)

6. Why does Frodo want the ring to be taken out of the Shire? (*He wants to protect his home from the dangerous power of the ring and those who seek it.*)

7. Why does Sauron allow Gollum to escape? (*He hopes that Gollum's desire for the ring will lead Sauron to whomever possesses the ring.*)

8. How do the hobbits escape from Old Man Willow? (*Tom Bombadil's singing persuades the tree to let them go.*)

9. What makes Tom Bombadil unique? (*The One Ring seems to have no effect on him.*)

10. Why does Frodo begin to trust Strider? (*The innkeeper Barliman Butterbur gives Frodo a letter from Gandalf, which reveals that Strider will help them reach Rivendell.*)

11. What are the consequences of Frodo's accidental disappearance at *The Prancing Pony*? (*Those who witness his disappearance realize his true identity and that he has the ring.*)

LITERARY ELEMENTS

12. Character: Gandalf considers the hobbits to be "amazing creatures." What is one example of his faith in Frodo? (*Gandalf doesn't feel the ring will have an effect on Frodo for some time.*) How might Gandalf's view of Frodo and the role he can play in this important journey contrast with traditional ideas of what a hero is? (*Traditional heroes are big, strong, and brave; Frodo is small and feels weak and scared.*)

PERSONAL RESPONSE

13. Gandalf believes that Frodo was chosen to bear the ring. Does Frodo take the ring of his own free will? What do you think this says about the idea of destiny? Explain whether you believe in destiny.

CROSS-CURRICULAR ACTIVITIES

WRITING: *Power of Song*
Review with students the power that Tom Bombadil seems to get from singing. Then ask: *If you could choose any power other than pure physical strength, what would it be, and why?* Have students describe how they would use their powers. Discuss the possibility that their powers might be used for evil.

HISTORY: *Medieval England*
The setting of *The Lord of the Rings* is very similar to Medieval England. Have students visit the library to research life during medieval times. Then groups can compare and contrast Medieval England and Tolkien's Middle-earth.

LANGUAGE ARTS: *Personification*
Personification occurs when a writer applies the traits of humans to inanimate objects. Challenge students to list the examples of personification they find in Book One. What kind of role do they think nature will play in *The Lord of the Rings*?

WHAT HAPPENS

Frodo wakes in Rivendell. He's over-joyed to see Gandalf and Bilbo and to learn that the rest of his group escaped the Black Riders. At Rivendell, Elrond convenes a council to decide the fate of the ring. Present at the council are Gandalf, Arwen Evenstar, Glóin, Bilbo, Boromir, Legolas, Gimli, and Strider (also known as Aragorn, heir to the throne of Gondor). Boromir says that Sauron plans to attack Gondor. Gandalf warns that the wizard Saruman also

seeks the ring and that the wizard betrayed and imprisoned him to try to get it. Frodo says that he will take the ring to Mt. Doom in Mordor and destroy it. Sam, Merry, Pippin, Gandalf, Legolas, Gimli, Aragorn, and Boromir will accompany him. As they travel to Mordor, they're attacked by Orcs and Balrog, the fierce monster of fire and shadow. Gandalf fights and kills the Balrog but is dragged into a deep chasm with the monster. The group mourns its great loss. Aragorn assumes leadership of the group. In Lothlórien, they meet Celeborn and Galadriel, lord and lady of the elves. Galadriel shows Sam and Frodo her magic mirror, which reveals past and future events. Frodo offers the ring to Galadriel, but she refuses it. Before going on to Mordor, Boromir insists the ring first be used to save Gondor. He accosts Frodo, who puts on the ring to escape. Seeing the power that the ring is beginning to have over members of his own group, Frodo decides to go to Mordor alone. Sam figures out Frodo's plan and insists on joining him. They float down the Anduin River in one of the elf boats.

QUESTIONS TO TALK ABOUT

COMPREHENSION AND RECALL

1. What races are represented at the gathering at Rivendell? *(elves, men, dwarves, and hobbits)*

2. What three things do Boromir and his brother Faramir see in their dream about Rivendell? *(a broken sword, a halfling, and the ring)*

3. How does the Company of the Ring discover what happened to Balin? *(In Moria, they find Balin's tomb and a manuscript that tells how he was killed by an Orc.)*

HIGHER-LEVEL THINKING SKILLS

4. What is the major purpose of the meeting at Rivendell? *(The council must decide what to do with the One Ring.)*

5. What plan of Sauron's does the council learn about? *(Sauron plans to attack Gondor.)*

6. What betrayal has Gandalf suffered? *(Saruman, a wizard from Gandalf's order, imprisoned Gandalf when he would not reveal information about the location of the ring.)*

7. What is Frodo's reaction when he realizes that he must take the ring to Mt. Doom? *(He is concerned and feels burdened, although he knows the decision is the right one.)*

8. What does Boromir seem to think about the warning about the ring? *(The warning about the evil power of the ring does not apply to righteous men.)*

9. What decision does Frodo's confrontation with Boromir prompt? *(Frodo believes that he must travel to Mordor alone.)*

LITERARY ELEMENTS

10. Structural Device: How do you think the quest undertaken in Book Two of *The Fellowship of the Ring* is similar to other famous literary or movie quests you have read about or seen? *(Possible answer, compared to* The Odyssey *or* The Iliad: *a long journey, facing monsters, hero must have strength of convictions and learn things about himself.)* How does it differ? *(Possible answer: This is not a quest for an object as in the movie* Indiana Jones and the Last Crusade. *Unlike Indiana Jones, Frodo's quest is to destroy the ring.)*

PERSONAL RESPONSE

11. Why do you think Frodo offers the One Ring to Galadriel? Are you surprised by her reaction? Explain your reasoning.

CROSS-CURRICULAR ACTIVITIES

SCIENCE: *Volcanoes!*
Only the fires of Orodruin can melt and destroy the One Ring. Have students learn more about volcanoes, including the following questions: *What makes volcanoes hot? How hot is the fire in a volcano? Can a volcano's fire melt stone or glass? At what temperatures do objects made of steel, gold, or rock melt?*

SOCIAL STUDIES: *Seeking Council*
All the races of Middle-earth are represented at the council meeting in Rivendell. Use this as a starting point for students to explore the idea of government representation. Have groups examine different forms of councils, or governing bodies, such as Congress, the United Nations, and even their own student council. How are decisions made in these organizations? How can an organization ensure the fair representation of all the different groups (grades, cultures, races) it governs?

WRITING: *Put to the Test*
Galadriel tests the hobbits with questions when she first meets them to find out more about their intentions. Instruct students to devise a test to determine whether someone would make a suitable best friend. What criteria can help determine what makes a good friend? Students may want to divide the criteria into different categories, such as interests, age, gender, personal beliefs, and so on. What requirements are mandatory? Are there any categories in which students are willing to make exceptions? How well do students think they would score on their own tests?

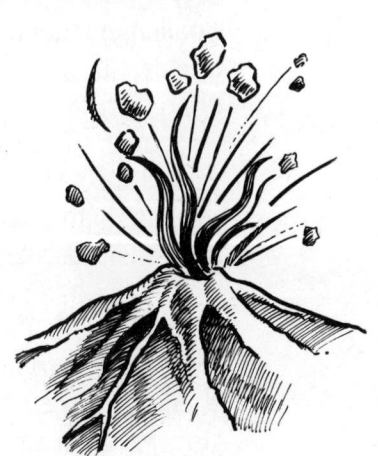

Summarizing *The Fellowship of the Ring*

Choose from among the activities below to help students summarize and appreciate *The Fellowship of the Ring*.

CLASS PROJECT: *Design a Quest*

Books One and Two of *The Fellowship of the Ring* begin with gatherings (a birthday party and the council at Rivendell) that signal the beginning of a journey or quest. Have the entire class or groups of students design a quest of their own. The quest could take them as close as the school library or it could be used to plan a year-end field trip. The final destination of the quest will determine what the students will be seeking. For example, the class might journey to the town or city museum. Students might design maps and give mythical names to some of the local landmarks that they may pass on the way. What obstacles will they face on their quest? What kind of transportation will they use? Will they need money for admission? Are there time constraints? Prepare a list of things for students to find at the museum (a picture of an animal, two maps, and so on).

GROUP PROJECT: *Council Meeting*

The purpose of the gathering at Rivendell is to decide the fate of the ring. Recreating this meeting in small groups will help students further understand the meeting's importance and the conflicting opinions about what should be done with the ring. Divide the class into groups. Assign a character who played a significant role in the meeting at Rivendell to each group member. Choose appropriate passages from the book for groups to read aloud and act out. Then have students put away their books and debate what should be done with the ring. Can it be used for good? Should it be destroyed? Emphasize that they must back up their opinions with facts. To make the debate even more dramatic, you may want to allow students to wear costumes as they act out their scenes.

PARTNER PROJECT: *Want Ads*

Challenge students to write want ads looking for heroes to go on very important quests. Samples from newspaper want ads can serve as structural guides. What characteristics and requirements should the hero have? What kind of experience? Are there any physical requirements? Remind students that size and outward appearance can often be deceptive, as in the case of the hobbits. Direct partners to exchange and discuss their ads. Encourage them to make revisions to their ads after their discussion. Then post the ads on a bulletin board.

INDIVIDUAL PROJECT: *What If . . . ?*

Tell students to imagine that they were given the magic ring of invisibility. Have them trace their hands on sheets of paper and then draw their rings on one of the fingers. Then ask students to describe what they would do—and wouldn't do—with their new power. Would they keep the existence of the ring a secret? How could they make sure the ring wasn't used for evil? Then have students design other objects with magical powers. What power did they choose and why?

EVALUATION IDEAS

Ask students to create a set of rubrics to assess one of the summarizing projects. For example, a rubric for the want-ad activity might include the following objectives:

• Is the information in the ad presented clearly?
• Does the ad read like a real want ad?
• Do students present valid reasons for the requirements they list in the ad?
• Do the want ads capture the sense of adventure involved in a quest?

Answers for Worksheets

page 12: 1. Sauron 2. Frodo 3. Boromir 4. Saruman 5. Gollum

page 13: Answers may vary. Be sure students write clear, descriptive reasons about the items, their reasons for giving them to specific people, and the items' personal importance.

page 14: Answers may vary. Possible: Galadriel's Crystal Phial; light source; works in the dark when others fail. Gandalf's Staff; use it to start fires and cast spells; can destroy bridges so watch where you stand. Tom Bombadil's Song; frees hobbits and other creatures from Old Man Willow; only works inside the Old Forest.

Name: _____

Ring Around the Ring

Each of the characters below has a special relationship to the ring. Write the name of each character next to the description of their relationship to the ring.

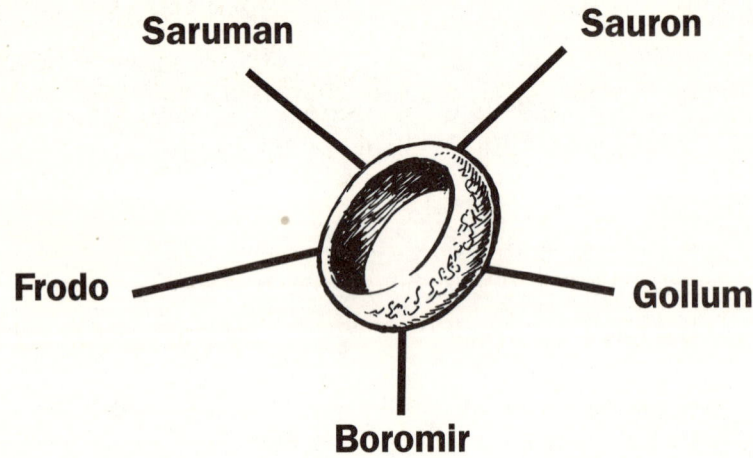

1. He made the ring. _____

2. He currently possesses the ring. _____

3. He wants to use the ring to save Gondor. _____

4. He betrays Gandalf and tries to get information about the location of the ring.

_____

5. He informs the Dark Lord of Mordor that a hobbit has the ring.

_____

6. On which character does the ring have the strongest effect? Explain your answer.

_____

Name: _____

Treasure Chest

At the beginning of *The Fellowship of the Ring*, Bilbo wants to give some of his possessions to Frodo. Imagine that you have a treasure chest filled with wonderful things from your life. You decide to distribute these things to friends and/or family members. Write about five items you would put in the chest and who would receive each one. What is the importance of each item to you?

Item	Given to	Importance of Item
1. _____ _____	_____ _____	_____ _____
2. _____ _____	_____ _____	_____ _____
3. _____ _____	_____ _____	_____ _____
4. _____ _____	_____ _____	_____ _____
5. _____ _____	_____ _____	_____ _____

Name: _____

Magical Mystical Jewelry Store

Imagine a store full of magical items from *The Fellowship of the Ring*. Display four magical items from Books One and Two in the store. Write the item's name, description of its power, and any special features or warnings to the buyer. Draw a picture of each item. The first one is done for you.

Full Moon SALE!

Seeing Stone SPECIAL

Item Name: The One Ring

Description of Power: Those who wear it become invisible.

Special Features or Warnings: Beware! The ring will eventually destroy whoever wears it!

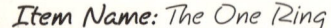

Exploring the Book

WHAT HAPPENS

As Frodo and Sam continue to Mordor alone, Orcs kill Boromir and capture Merry and Pippin. Aragorn, Gimli, and Legolas search for Merry and Pippin. The two hobbits manage to escape and are eventually sheltered by Treebeard. In their search for Merry and Pippin, Aragorn and the others meet an old man who speaks in riddles. The old man is Gandalf, who has passed through death and is now more powerful. Gandalf travels with Aragorn, Gimli, and Legolas to Edoras. Théoden rules Edoras and has been influenced by Saruman's servant Wormtongue. Wormtongue is banished after Gandalf breaks his hold over Théoden, who then leads a defense of the Rohan stronghold, Helm's Deep. Théoden goes on to attack the Orcs of Isengard and finds that Isengard has already been destroyed by Treebeard and the Ents. There, the group is reunited with Merry and Pippin. Saruman is in Orthanc, the tower at the center of Isengard, and Gandalf tries to talk sense to the once wise wizard. When Saruman resists, Gandalf breaks Saruman's staff. In anger, Wormtongue mistakenly throws a palantir (seeing-stone) out of the window, thereby giving it to Gandalf. Pippin steals a peek at the stone, revealing himself to Sauron, who mistakenly thinks Pippin has been captured by Saruman. Gandalf tells Théoden and Aragorn to return to Helm's Deep. He and Pippin continue on to Minas Tirith in Gondor.

QUESTIONS TO TALK ABOUT

COMPREHENSION AND RECALL

1. Where did the man who speaks in riddles come from? *(It is Gandalf. He has passed through death and has returned from destroying the Balrog.)*

2. Why kind of funeral did Aragorn, Gimli, and Legolas hold for Boromir? *(They placed his body and weapons in a boat and floated it down the Anduin.)*

3. Who is Treebeard? *(Treebeard is the oldest living thing in Middle-earth.)*

HIGHER-LEVEL THINKING SKILLS

4. What is the significance of Grima's name, Wormtongue? *(He is a traitor. The name implies that his speech is deceptive. His tongue squirms like a worm.)*

5. How does Saruman first respond to Gandalf's attempts to change his mind about the ring? *(Saruman tries to use his powers of persuasive speech on Théoden and Gandalf to convince them to see things his way.)*

6. What is the importance of Gandalf's breaking the staff of Saruman? *(He destroys Saruman's sign of authority.)*

7. What are the consequences of Wormtongue's anger? *(In his rage, he throws a large object out of the window at them. It is a seeing stone, which will be useful to Gandalf, and is now out of the hands of his master Saruman.)*

8. Why is it better that Pippin, and not Gandalf, uses the seeing stone first? *(Sauron remains unaware of Gandalf's presence.)*

9. What does Sauron assume when he sees Pippin in the seeing stone? *(Sauron thinks that Pippin has been captured by Saruman.)*

10. Why does Gandalf hand over the stone over to Aragorn? *(Since Aragorn is the last of the line of the kings of Gondor, the stone belongs to him.)*

LITERARY ELEMENTS

11. Symbolism: What two major symbols are featured in Book Three? *(staff of Saruman, seeing stone)* What does each symbol represent? *(Staff: Saruman's authority as chief of the order of wizards. Seeing stone: Aragorn's right to the throne of Gondor.)*

12. Conflict and Character: What are the similarities and differences between Gandalf and Saruman? *(Both wise and powerful, both wizards in the same order, both want the ring. Saruman wants the ring for power, Gandalf wants the ring to be destroyed. Gandalf does not want to be corrupted by the ring, Saruman believes the power could be used for good but wants the strength the ring can give him.)*

PERSONAL RESPONSE

13. If you had the opportunity, would you use a seeing stone to look into the future? What might be the advantages and disadvantages of knowing what was going to happen? If you could choose one thing about your future to know about, what would it be and why?

CROSS-CURRICULAR ACTIVITIES

MATH: *Length of a League*
The characters in *The Lord of the Rings* use leagues to measure distance. Challenge students to find out how long a league is. Then ask them to convert some of the distances described in the book from leagues to miles and to explain how they did so. Students may also want to try to guess the length (in feet) of Treebeard's stride. Then they can estimate how many feet and miles he traveled with Pippin and Merry.

ART: *Seeing Stones*
Have students collect their own seeing stones and bring them to class. Stones can be found anywhere, and students may decorate them using paint or natural materials. This activity can be done on an individual basis or as part of a class field trip to a local park or nature area. Direct students to write brief descriptions about their stones and what appealed to them about the stones' appearances.

LANGUAGE ARTS: *What's in a Name?*
Let students work in pairs to discuss the titles of the chapters in Book Three. What do they think the titles refer to specifically and/or symbolically? Ask each pair to share their conclusions with the rest of the class. Discuss their different theories about Tolkien's choice of chapter titles.

WHAT HAPPENS

While other powers prepare for war, Frodo and Sam continue toward Mordor. Along the way, they capture Gollum and force him to guide them to Mordor. Hoping to steal the ring from Frodo, Gollum agrees. When they are unable to enter through the Black Gate of Mordor, Gollum takes them to the pass Cirith Ugol. While temporarily separated from Gollum, Frodo and Sam are captured by Gondorians led by Faramir, Boromir's brother and Denethor's son. After a brief battle with the men who serve the Dark Lord, Faramir takes Frodo and Sam to a safe place. Faramir learns of his brother's death and finds out about the existence of the ring from Sam. Gollum is captured by Faramir's men and 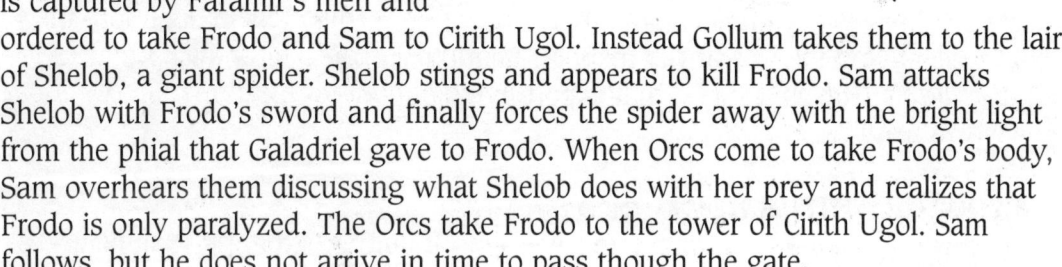 ordered to take Frodo and Sam to Cirith Ugol. Instead Gollum takes them to the lair of Shelob, a giant spider. Shelob stings and appears to kill Frodo. Sam attacks Shelob with Frodo's sword and finally forces the spider away with the bright light from the phial that Galadriel gave to Frodo. When Orcs come to take Frodo's body, Sam overhears them discussing what Shelob does with her prey and realizes that Frodo is only paralyzed. The Orcs take Frodo to the tower of Cirith Ugol. Sam follows, but he does not arrive in time to pass though the gate.

QUESTIONS TO TALK ABOUT

COMPREHENSION AND RECALL

1. Who do Frodo and Sam capture, and what do they do with their prisoner? *(They capture Gollum and force him to lead them to Mordor.)*

2. Where does Gollum first take Sam and Frodo when they arrive at Mordor? *(Gollum takes them to the Black Gate of Mordor.)*

HIGHER-LEVEL THINKING SKILLS

3. Why are the marshes that Sam, Gollum, and Frodo cross called the Dead Marshes? *(The Dead Marshes contain the bodies of men, Orcs, and elves that have been killed in battle.)*

4. What piece of information is accidentally revealed while Sam and Frodo are with Faramir? *(Sam lets Faramir know about the presence of the ring.)*

5. Why does Gollum lead Frodo and Sam to Shelob? *(He hopes that Shelob will kill them but will be uninterested in the ring, so he can then take it for himself.)*

6. What causes Shelob to eventually back away from Sam? *(Sam uses Galadriel's phial, and the bright light causes Shelob to back off.)*

7. What gives Sam the courage to attack Shelob? *(He is angry that Shelob has killed his good friend.)*

8. How does Sam realize that Frodo is paralyzed? *(As the Orcs move to take Frodo's body, Sam overhears them discussing what Shelob does with her prey.)*

LITERARY ELEMENTS

9. Mood: What is the mood at the end of Book Four? *(Possible: Sad and morbid because of the attack on Frodo; relief that Frodo is not dead; foreboding and suspenseful when Sam is unable to follow the Orcs through the gate to find out where they are taking Frodo.)*

PERSONAL RESPONSE

10. Sam abandons his responsibility to the ring to go after Frodo. Is he is right to do this? What are the benefits or drawbacks of his choice? What would you have done?

CROSS-CURRICULAR ACTIVITIES

SCIENCE: *Arachnophobia!*
Shelob is a giant spider with a powerful sting. Have students research different types of spiders. Which spiders are the most dangerous? What kinds of spiders are found in your area? They should also discuss the beneficial role that spiders play. Ask them to talk about the images that they commonly associate with spiders. You might want to mention Charlotte in *Charlotte's Web* as a spider that is portrayed in a positive way.

LANGUAGE ARTS: *Ancient Sayings*
Sam cries out in an elvish tongue to save himself during battle. J.R.R. Tolkien studied languages all his life and created his own languages for his books. Many of our slogans and sayings come from ancient languages, for example, *E Pluribus Unum* ("out of many, one") and *Temet Nosce* ("know thyself") come from Latin. Pair students and direct them to find proverbs and sayings from ancient languages, such as Latin or Greek, that we still use today.

LITERARY COMPARISON: *The Buddy System*
Sam and Frodo have become partners on this adventure. Have the class discuss other partners that they have encountered in other books or learned about in history. Ask students to brainstorm similarities and differences between the relationships those partners exhibit and the relationship between Frodo and Sam.

Summarizing
The Two Towers

Choose from among the following activities to help students summarize and appreciate *The Two Towers*.

CLASS PROJECT: *Middle-earth Collage*

Explain that a collage is a picture created by putting together different materials, such as photographs, pieces of newspaper and magazines, and other objects on a piece of paper. Have students create their own collages to represent some of the places and images in Books Three and Four. For instance, what do they think Mordor or the Dead Marshes look like? How do they visualize the forest or Shelob's lair? Supply various materials including newspapers, magazines, sticks, leaves, cloth, and other materials for students to use.

GROUP PROJECT: *Words-worth*

During his life, Tolkien studied languages and devised letters and sounds and symbols for the worlds he created in his books. Challenge small groups of students to make up languages of their own. Each group should provide a name for its language and create an alphabet and five words to present to the rest of the class. Ask students to explain why they chose the letters and symbols they used. For instance, do the sounds of the words in the new language remind them of the objects the words describe? In preparation for this exercise, you may want to provide examples of different alphabets, such as Norwegian, Welsh, Greek, Japanese, Arabic, and point out the different letters and symbols used in each alphabet. You may also want to talk about the use of symbols in hieroglyphics.

PARTNER PROJECT: *Riddle Me This*

When Gandalf reappears in Book Three, he is disguised in rags and speaks in riddles. Have students work with partners to make up riddles that describe people, places, or things. They can use the riddles to describe where they were born, their favorite animals or sports teams—or something more commonplace, such as a toaster or a garden hose. The riddles should be composed of short descriptive sentences. For example, to describe a toaster, students might write the following: *It's both hot and cold. It works when it's down. It gets up when it's done.*

INDIVIDUAL PROJECT: *Trading Cards*

Have students pick two of their favorite characters from *The Lord of the Rings* and make trading cards for them. Discuss with the class which information would be important to include, such as special talents or traits, strengths and weaknesses, age, physical descriptions, and/or goals and motives. The cards can be made out of poster board, construction paper, or index cards. Students may paint, draw, or use images from magazines or newspaper to illustrate their cards. Post trading cards in the classroom, and set up a time for trading them. Also, make the cards available as study guides for groups.

EVALUATION IDEAS
Ask students to create a set of rubrics to assess one of the summarizing projects. A rubric used to critique the trading cards project might include the following objectives:
• Does each card include enough information about a character?
• Is the information accurate, and does it show an understanding of the character?
• Are the cards well-written and organized clearly?
• Do the cards present information creatively?

ANSWERS FOR WORKSHEETS
Page 21: 2. Boromir is the brother of Faramir. 3. Glóin is the father of Gimli. 4. Tom Bombadil is the husband of Goldberry. 5. Elrond is the father of Arwen Evenstar. 6. Théoden is the uncle of Eomer. 7. Faramir is the son of Denethor.

Page 22: The order is as follows: 1. Boromir dies. 2. Merry and Pippin escape from the Orcs. 3. Gandalf reappears. 4. Gandalf breaks Saruman's staff. 5. Pippin looks into the seeing stone. 6. Gollum takes the hobbits to the Dead Marshes. 7. Sam sees the Oliphaunts. 8. Faramir's men capture Gollum. 9. Frodo is stung by Shelob. 10. Orcs take Frodo's body to the tower of Cirith Ugol. Students' favorite events and sequence of events may vary.

Page 23: Answers may vary. Possible: Things associated with Earth: army of trees, seeing stones; Things associated with Fire: Balrog; the volcano's power to destroy the ring; Things associated with Water: Galadriel's basin; Goldberry's power to create rain. Animals: Gwaihir, Lord of Eagles rescued Gandalf twice; the legendary horse Shadowfax helped Gandalf speed across the country; Shelob the Spider paralyzed Frodo.

Name: _____

All in the Family

There are many special relationships between the characters in *The Lord of the Rings*. Describe the relationship between each pair of characters below. The first one is done for you.

1. Bilbo and Frodo are __cousins__.

2. Boromir and Faramir are _____.

3. Glóin and Gimli are _____.

4. Tom Bombadil and Goldberry are _____.

5. Elrond and Arwen Evenstar are _____.

6. Théoden and Eomer are _____.

7. Faramir and Denethor are _____.

Time for Timelines

In which order have the following
10 events occurred in the book?
Number the events from 1–10.

_____ Pippin looks into the seeing stone.

_____ Orcs take Frodo's body to the tower
of Cirith Ugol.

_____ Gandalf breaks Saruman's staff.

_____ Sam sees the Oliphaunts.

_____ Frodo is stung by Shelob.

_____ Faramir's men capture Gollum.

_____ Gandalf reappears.

_____ Gollum takes the hobbits to the Dead Marshes.

_____ Boromir dies.

_____ Merry and Pippin escape from the Orcs.

1. List three of your favorite events from *The Two Towers* that are not listed above.

_____

_____

_____

2. Where would each of your favorite events fit among the 10 events above? Write a new list on a separate sheet of paper. Place all the events—including your three events—in the correct order.

3. Which event is your favorite—and why?

_____

_____

_____

It's Elemental

In *The Lord of the Rings,* there are many different characters of all shapes, sizes, and origin. Nature plays a very important role in Middle-earth. For each of the elements named below, list a character, symbol, or power from the book that is associated with the element.

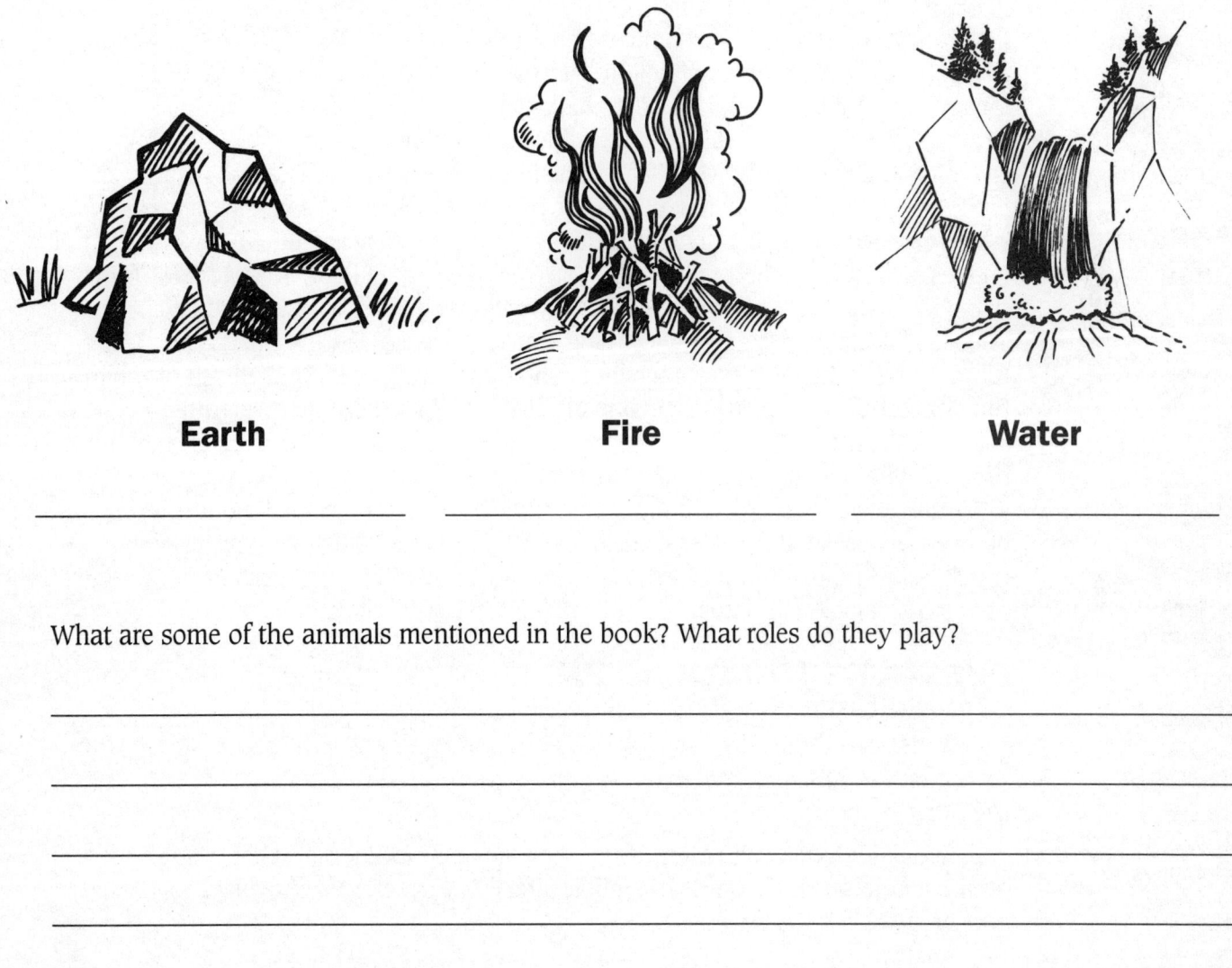

Earth   **Fire**   **Water**

_____   _____   _____

What are some of the animals mentioned in the book? What roles do they play?

_____

_____

_____

_____

_____

_____

Exploring the Book

THE RETURN OF THE KING: BOOK FIVE

WHAT HAPPENS

Gandalf and Pippin arrive at Minas Tirith in Gondor where Denethor hears of Boromir's death. Preparing to join Théoden, Aragorn receives a staff from Arwen and a message from Elrond about the Paths of the Dead. Instead of going to meet Théoden, Aragorn decides to take the paths in order to reach Minas Tirith more quickly. He first goes to the Stone of Erech and asks the Dead to join him, allowing them to fulfill the oath of loyalty to Isildur they broke long ago. Following

Aragorn frees them from eternal unrest. Meanwhile, Théoden gets a message from Denethor to ride to Gondor and help in the battle. When Denethor learns Faramir let Frodo and Sam go without first obtaining the ring, he sends his son to a dangerous post where Faramir is badly wounded. Distraught, Denethor makes a funeral pyre for himself and his son. Théoden and the Rohirrim arrive to join in the fight. Merry, barred from riding into battle with them, travels secretly with a rider who calls himself Dernhelm. Théoden falls under his horse after being struck by the Lord of the Nazgûl, chief of the Ringwraiths. Dernhelm attacks the lord, who claims that no living man can hurt him. But Dernhelm is a woman—Eowyn in disguise—and she kills him. Aragorn arrives by ship with the army of the Dead. The battle is won. Gandalf saves Faramir's body from the pyre, but Denethor jumps onto the flames with one of the palantir. The group travels to Mordor to face Sauron. Arriving at the Black Gate, they're greeted by the Lieutenant of the Tower of Barad-dûr. He produces evidence of Frodo's capture, which Gandalf seizes. Attackers exit through the Black Gate. In an attempt to save his friend Beregond from a troll, Pippin falls under the monster and loses consciousness.

QUESTIONS TO TALK ABOUT

COMPREHENSION AND RECALL

1. What two things do the elf princes bring to Aragorn? *(They bring a staff from Arwen and a message from Elrond reminding Aragorn to remember the Paths of the Dead.)*

2. When Théoden asks Merry to accompany him to Edoras, what gesture of gratitude and servitude does the hobbit offer? *(Merry gives his sword to Théoden and becomes his squire.)*

3. Why doesn't Aragorn go to meet Théoden? *(He decides to take the Paths of the Dead and ask the Dead to follow him. This would fulfill the once-broken oath that has cursed them and thus free them from eternal unrest.)*

HIGHER-LEVEL THINKING SKILLS

4. Why does Pippin offer his services to Denethor? *(Pippin wishes to make up for the death of Denethor's son, Boromir.)*

5. What does Aragorn hope to accomplish by revealing himself to Sauron? *(Aragorn hopes to raise doubts in Sauron's mind by showing him Elendil, the sword that defeated Sauron long ago and that Aragorn now carries.)*

6. Why does Eowyn beg Aragorn not to go down the Paths of the Dead? *(It is said the living never return from the Paths of the Dead.)*

7. How does Denethor react when he learns that Faramir let Sam and Frodo go? *(He is angry and disappointed that Faramir did not get the ring from them and bring it to him.)*

8. Why isn't the victory at Minas Tirith a final one? *(Sauron's forces must still be faced.)*

9. What is the significance of Aragorn's healing power? *(It is a sign that he is a true king, because true kings have the power to heal.)*

10. How does the Lieutenant of the Tower of Barad-dûr prove that Frodo has been captured? *(He produces the coat of mail, brooch, and cloak worn by Frodo.)*

LITERARY ELEMENTS

11. Foreshadowing: Gandalf reminds Denethor of the prophecy that claims the Lord of the Nazgûl, chief of the Ringwraiths, will not die by the hand of man. What event does this foreshadow? *(The destruction of the Lord of the Nazgûl by a woman—Eowyn.)*

PERSONAL RESPONSE

12. Gandalf tells the Company that they will be walking directly into a trap when they go to face Sauron, but that they must do it. Why is it sometimes necessary to face a difficult situation, even one that makes you afraid? Tell of a time when you had to face something difficult and were glad that you did.

13. The Dead were cursed because they broke a pledge. They say they broke it because circumstances had changed. Explain whether you feel it is ever right to break a pledge. Support your answer with examples.

CROSS-CURRICULAR ACTIVITIES

ART: *Flags Are Flying!*
The emblem on the flags of the ships that Aragorn sailed into battle belong to the house of Eladil. Have students design flags or banners that represent their families, class, school, or teams. What do the symbols on their flags represent, and why did students choose those particular emblems?

SCIENCE: *Plant Power*
Aragorn uses herbs to heal the wounded. Ask groups of students to find out how herbs are used today to heal different ailments. They may use sources from the library and/or the Internet. Encourage students to use their results to make an herbal first aid chart that can be posted in class.

WRITING AND LITERATURE: *The Role of Women*
Eowyn is able to destroy the Lord of the Nazgûl because she is a woman. Have students write paragraphs about what the role of women has been up to this point in *The Lord of the Rings.* To extend the discussion, you may want to challenge them to compare the roles of women in this book to other books they have read in class.

WHAT HAPPENS

At the gate of the Tower of Cirith Ugol, Sam puts on the ring temporarily while he tries to find an entrance. Finally, he uses the Phial of Galadriel to enter. Sam rescues Frodo, and the two go further into Mordor, disguised in Orc uniforms. They are attacked by Gollum when they reach Mt. Doom. Frodo goes ahead. Sam wounds Gollum but cannot bring himself to kill the creature. Frodo, unable to throw the ring into the flames, puts it on. Gollum reaches Frodo and bites off his ring finger. Thrilled that he has reclaimed the ring, Gollum falls into the volcano. Sauron loses power when the ring is destroyed, and the armies of Mordor retreat from the battle at the Black Gate. At Minas Tirith in the Houses of the Healing, Faramir plans to marry Eowyn. He acknowledges Aragorn as true king, and Aragorn, who weds Arwen Evenstar, is given responsibility for the care of Middle-earth by Gandalf. After attending Théoden's funeral, Gandalf and the hobbits head home. Along the way, they meet Saruman—now a beggar—and Wormtongue. At Rivendell, Bilbo gives his papers to his cousin so Frodo can continue to write the history of their adventures. Now disguised as a man called Sharkey, Saruman is creating trouble in the Shire. At the Battle of Bywater, the hobbits save the Shire. After Frodo spares Saruman's life, the wizard betrays Wormtongue, who then kills Saruman and runs away. The restoration of the damaged Shire begins. Sam marries Rosie Cotton, and they live with and care for Frodo. On the anniversary of his and Bilbo's birthdays, Frodo passes the history to Sam. Frodo and Sam leave the Shire to go to the Grey Havens, where Gandalf waits to take Frodo toward the Blessed Realm. Merry and Pippin, who are also at the Havens, return with Sam to the Shire.

HOME SWEET HOME

QUESTIONS TO TALK ABOUT

COMPREHENSION AND RECALL

1. Why does Sam put on the ring? *(He is searching for an entrance into the Tower.)*

2. How do Sam and Frodo make their way into Mordor? *(They disguise themselves in Orc uniforms.)*

3. What happens at Mt. Doom? *(Gollum surprises Frodo and Sam and tries to take the ring.)*

HIGHER-LEVEL THINKING SKILLS

4. Why are the Orcs frightened of Sam? *(His shadow makes him appear to be very large.)*

5. Why doesn't Sam kill Gollum when he has the chance? *(Sam feels pity for him.)*

6. What happens to Frodo when he gets to the brink of the volcano? *(He is overcome by the power of the ring and cannot bring himself to throw it in. He puts on the ring.)*

7. How is the ring finally destroyed? *(Gollum falls into the volcano with the ring.)*

8. What warning is fulfilled when Gollum falls into the flames? *(The one who bears the ring will be destroyed by it.)*

9. What happens when the ring melts? *(Sauron's powers are weakened, and his army retreats.)*

10. What are the consequences of Arwen's marriage to Aragorn? *(Arwen will no longer be immune to natural death.)*

11. Why does Wormtongue kill Saruman? *(Saruman betrays Wormtongue by revealing that he killed Lotho.)*

LITERARY ELEMENTS

12. Foreshadowing: On the journey back to the Shire, the wound that Frodo suffered one year earlier at Weathertop is particularly painful. What does this foreshadow? *(Saruman foretells that Frodo will not have a long life or enjoy good health.)*

PERSONAL RESPONSE

13. Were you surprised when Frodo was unable to throw the ring into the volcano? Explain your answer.

CROSS-CURRICULAR ACTIVITIES

SCIENCE: *Trees, Please*
A great deal of the damage suffered by the Shire was environmental, especially in the form of deforestation. How has deforestation affected the United States and other parts of the world? Ask students to research the long-term consequences of losing forests. You might also have them find out more about Arbor Day and how they can participate in tree plantings in the area.

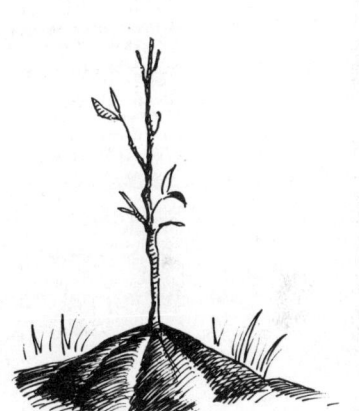

WRITING AND HISTORY: *Tolkien's World*
J.R.R. Tolkien served in World War I, lived in England, and studied languages all his life. Encourage students to explore the time during which Tolkien lived and write paragraphs about the ways in which the world the writer grew up in is represented in the world he created in *The Lord of the Rings*.

ART: *Picturing the Blessed Realm*
At the end of *The Lord of the Rings*, Frodo is taken toward the Blessed Realm. Have students draw maps of what lands they think Frodo will pass through along the way. Also ask them to sketch pictures of what they think the Blessed Realm looks like. Post the maps and pictures, and discuss the variations in students' interpretations.

Summarizing
The Return of the Kings

Choose from among the following activities to help students summarize and appreciate *The Return of the King*.

CLASS PROJECT: *The Daily Shire*

Assign the task of putting out a newsletter that describes what has been taking place in and around the Shire. Provide several examples of newspapers and newsletters for students to study. The class can be split into groups who act as reporters to cover different aspects of the book. The newsletter can include interviews with characters, detailed accounts of what happens in a particular scene or during a specific battle, and maps showing the Company's progress in their quest. In addition to fact-based articles, there can also be more lighthearted pieces that encourage creative writing, such as "Sam's Gardening Tips," "Hobbits' Habits," and so on. Students can also include ads, illustrations, and announcements. After all the separate elements have been completed, have the class brainstorm headlines and decide what the important front-page stories will be. If possible, print copies of the newsletter to distribute to the class for use as a study guide.

PARTNER PROJECT: *Look to the Future*

Prophecies and curses are uttered throughout *The Lord of the Rings*. Examples include the following: *the Dark Rider can never be killed by the hand of a man; the dream of Faramir and Boromir of the three things that would be found at Rivendell; Galadriel's magic mirror; Pippin looks into the seeing stone.* Have students work with partners to make their own predictions about what will happen during the rest of the school year. Use a box or container as a time capsule in which partners place their predictions. Discuss with students how they feel about prophecies and fortunetellers. How much importance do they think destiny and free will play in a person's life? At the end of the year, open the time capsule and read aloud students' predictions.

INDIVIDUAL PROJECT: *A World All Your Own*

Most editions of *The Lord of the Rings* include several appendices that contain a vast amount of information about the world that J.R.R. Tolkien created including the history leading up to the time of the War of the Ring, calendars, and language and alphabets. Challenge students to create a fantasy world of their own. Before beginning this project, discuss aspects that might be important to include, such as the following: *What is the name of this land? What kind of government does it have? What races inhabit this land? What language(s) do they speak? What kind of calendar or clocks do they use? Does this land exist in the past, present, or future?* Ask students to describe a typical day in their world. Additionally, you may have them produce maps of their lands and timelines of important historical events and people.

INDIVIDUAL PROJECT: *History of Your Times*

Bilbo wants his cousin Frodo to continue writing the history of their times. Frodo then passes on this charge to his friend Sam. Encourage students to write their own family histories. They can begin by conducting interviews with as many family members as possible. Before students begin the interviews, guide them in preparing a list of questions that will yield information. Emphasize that they should gather as much specific data as possible— dates, locations, names, and momentous events in the history of their family. Students can also construct timelines showing important dates, such as marriages, births, deaths, moves, new schools, and personal achievements.

Name

Where were you born?

When were you born?

How many people were in your family?

What is your earliest memory?

EVALUATION IDEAS

Ask students to create a set of rubrics to assess one of the summarizing projects. A rubric used to critique the Shire newsletter might include the following objectives:

• Is the article written clearly and accurately? Is it understandable to the reader?
• Does the article contain important information that tells *who*, *what*, *where*, *when*, and *why*?
• How does the article compare to an article in your local newspaper?
• Have the articles been proofread and corrected?

ANSWERS FOR WORKSHEETS

Page 30: Lines should connect the following names: Saruman and Sharkey, Sméagol and Gollum, Dernhelm and Eowyn, Grima and Wormtongue, Strider and Aragorn, Peregrin Took and Pippin, Meriadoc Brandybuck and Merry.

Page 31: Answers may vary. Be sure students provide accurate information about the characters that they are comparing to themselves.

Page 32: Answers may vary. Possible: From *The Lord of the Rings:* Light—light from Gandalf's staff; light blazing from Galadriel's phial; White Council/Dark—Gandalf tells Balrog to go back to the Shadow; Dark Tower; Black Riders; Dark Lord. From Modern-day sayings: Light—reasons were brought to light; light of my life; light at the end of the tunnel; light the way/Dark—dark mood; dark times; dark ages; keeping someone in the dark/Colors: red—anger, stop; green—money, go; yellow—sun, wait.

What's in a Name?

Many of the characters in *The Lord of the Rings* are referred to by more than one name. Draw a line connecting the names that refer to the same character.

Saruman

Sméagol   **Gollum**

                    Merry

Dernhelm   **Wormtongue**

Aragorn   **Grima**

Strider   **Meriadoc Brandybuck**

Peregrin Took

Pippin   **Eowyn**

                    Sharkey

Do you have a nickname? What is it, and how did you get it?

_____

_____

_____

_____

Name: _____

Just Like Me

Choose a character from *The Lord of the Rings* that you like or admire. Think of what it is about that character that appeals to you. In what ways are you and the character similar? How are you different? Fill in the Venn diagram below to show the similarities and differences between you and the character.

Character Name: _____   Your Name: _____

BOTH

What do you admire about the character? _____

_____

What do you think the character would admire about you? _____

_____

Dark and Light

In *The Lord of the Rings*, Sauron is called the "Dark Lord." J.R.R. Tolkien uses the words *dark* and *light* throughout the book to create different moods or to indicate good or evil. List other examples of the symbolic use of *dark* and *light* in *The Lord of the Rings*.

From *The Lord of the Rings*

DARK

LIGHT

_____   _____
_____   _____
_____   _____
_____   _____
_____   _____

Now list examples of sayings in English that use the words *dark* and *light* to describe specific moods or feelings.

Modern-Day Sayings

DARK

LIGHT

_____   _____
_____   _____
_____   _____
_____   _____
_____   _____

AS A CLASS: Now that you've thought about what *dark* and *light* can mean, think about specific colors. Which colors are used to describe certain feelings or moods? On a separate sheet of paper, make a list of those colors and what they can symbolize.